CHOP IT UP
Vegan Style
WITH CHEF E.B.

VEGAN RECIPE PACK

E.B. JORDAN

AuthorHouse™
1663 Liberty Drive
Bloomington, IN 47403
www.authorhouse.com
Phone: 833-262-8899

Because of the dynamic nature of the Internet, any web addresses or links contained in this book may have changed since publication and may no longer be valid. The views expressed in this work are solely those of the author and do not necessarily reflect the views of the publisher, and the publisher hereby disclaims any responsibility for them.

This book is printed on acid-free paper.

ISBN: 979-8-8230-3519-4 (sc)
ISBN: 979-8-8230-3520-0 (hc)
ISBN: 979-8-8230-3518-7 (e)

Library of Congress Control Number: 2024921162

Print information available on the last page.

Published by AuthorHouse 10/28/2024

authorHOUSE®

with Chef E.B.

VEGAN
RECIPE PACK

Discover the collection of simple vegan recipes, including breakfast, lunch, dinner, treats and smoothie options.

chopitveganstyle@gmail.com

TABLE OF CONTENTS

Chop it up
Vegan Style
with Chef E.B.

TABLE OF CONTENTS

RECIPE KEY

Look for these helpful
icons throughout the file.

GF Gluten Free

DF Dairy Free

LC Low Carb (under 20g serving)

MP Meal Prep/Freezer Friendly

HP High Protein (over 20g per serving)

V Vegetarian

Q Quick (under 30 mins)

N Contains Nuts

WEEKLY MEAL PLANNER 01

	MONDAY	TUESDAY	WEDNESDAY	THURSDAY	FRIDAY	SATURDAY	SUNDAY
BREAKFAST	Greek Chickpeas on Toast	Banana Breakfast Oak	Green Pea & Mint Dip	Banana & Almond Muffins	Chickpea Scramble	Banana & Strawberry Pancakes	Protein Berry Smoothie Bowl
LUNCH	Quinoa Tabbouleh	Green Beans & Cherry Tomato Salad	Potato & Sundried Tomato Salad	Vegan 'Tuna' Salad	Sweet Potato, Quinoa & Bean Burger	Wild Rice, Tomato & Rocket Balsamic Salad	Garlic Zucchini &Tomato Pasta
SNACK	Green Pea & Mint Dip	Sundried Tomato Hummus	Banana & Almond Muffins	Matcha Enery Balls	Simple Vegan Oat Cookies	Energy Balls	Vegan Nutella
DINNER	Wild Rice, Tomato & Rocket Balsamic Salad	Red Sweet Potato Curry	Garlic Zucchini & Tomato Pasta	Tofu Pad Thai	Roasted Aubergine and Tomato Stew	Meal Out – Enjoy!	Sesame Tempeh Stir-Fry

WEEKLY SHOPPING LIST 01

FRUIT & VEGETABLES

Fresh
- ○ 2x shallots
- ○ 1x bulb garlic
- ○ 5x bananas
- ○ 2x lemons
- ○ strawberries
- ○ 1x avocado
- ○ 2x tomatoes
- ○ 1x cucumber
- ○ 2x bell peppers
- ○ 1x red onion
- ○ 1x white onion
- ○ 3x limes
- ○ 2x sweet potatoes
- ○ 2x zucchinis
- ○ 2x box cherry tomatoes
- ○ ginger
- ○ 2x carrots
- ○ 1x broccoli
- ○ rocket

Frozen
- ○ red berries
- ○ green peas

Herbs
- ○ 2x bunches parsley
- ○ 2x bunches mint
- ○ 1x bunch coriander
- ○ chives

NON-DAIRY & CONDIMENTS

Non-Dairy
- ○ almond milk
- ○ coconut milk
- ○ coconut yogurt
- ○ vegan parmesan
- ○ tempeh

Cans & Condiments
- ○ 2x cans chopped tomatoes
- ○ 2x cans chickpeas
- ○ black olives
- ○ maple syrup
- ○ vegan mayo
- ○ sweetcorn
- ○ natural peanut butter
- ○ almond butter
- ○ coconut milk (light)
- ○ rice wine vinegar
- ○ tamari
- ○ roasted peppers
- ○ balsamic vinegar
- ○ _____
- ○ _____
- ○ _____
- ○ _____
- ○ _____
- ○ _____
- ○ _____

GRAINS, SEEDS & BAKING

Grains
- ○ quinoa
- ○ white rice
- ○ wild rice mix
- ○ brown rice
- ○ brown rice pasta
- ○ porridge oats

Nuts & Seeds
- ○ peanuts
- ○ sesame seeds
- ○ chia seeds
- ○ walnuts
- ○ roasted almonds
- ○ dates

Baking
- ○ spelt flour
- ○ oat flour
- ○ baking powder
- ○ baking soda
- ○ almond meal
- ○ desiccated coconut
- ○ _____
- ○ _____
- ○ _____
- ○ _____
- ○ _____
- ○ _____
- ○ _____

SPICES & MISC.

Spices
- ○ smoked paprika
- ○ paprika
- ○ chili flakes
- ○ dried parsley

Oils
- ○ olive oil
- ○ coconut oil
- ○ sesame oil

Sweeteners
- ○ brown sugar
- ○ maple syrup

Other
- ○ bread
- ○ vegan vanilla protein powder
- ○ nori
- ○ Thai red curry paste
- ○ vegetable stock cubes
- ○ _____
- ○ _____
- ○ _____
- ○ _____
- ○ _____
- ○ _____
- ○ _____

Chop it up
Vegan Style
with Chef E.B.

WEEKLY MEAL PLANNER 02

MONDAY	TUESDAY	WEDNESDAY	THURSDAY	FRIDAY	SATURDAY	SUNDAY
BREAKFAST Chickpea Scramble	**BREAKFAST** Breakfast Oat Cookies	**BREAKFAST** Protein Berry Smoothie Bowl	**BREAKFAST** Carrot Pancakes with Almond Caramel	**BREAKFAST** Banana Breakfast Oats	**BREAKFAST** Banana & Strawberry Pancakes	**BREAKFAST** Breakfast Oat Cookies
LUNCH Green Beans & Cherry Tomato Salad	**LUNCH** Curried Tofu Salad	**LUNCH** Roasted Sweet Potato, Kale & Quinoa Salad	**LUNCH** Aubergine & Tomato Pasta	**LUNCH** Potato & Sundried Tomato Salad	**LUNCH** Quinoa Tabbouleh	**LUNCH** Sweet Potato, Quinoa & Bean Burger
SNACK Baba Ghanoush	**SNACK** Workout Chocolate Protein Smoothie	**SNACK** Roasted Miso Potatoes	**SNACK** Green Pea & Mint Dip	**SNACK** Post Workout Oat Banana Smoothie	**SNACK** Vegan Nutella	**SNACK** Sundried Tomato Hummus
DINNER Veg & Tahini Tray Bake	**DINNER** Sweet Potato & Bean Bake	**DINNER** Sesame Tempeh Stir –Fry	**DINNER** Spicy Cauliflower & Chickpea Rice Bowl	**DINNER** Quick Vegetable Stir Fry	**DINNER** Meal Out – Enjoy!	**DINNER** Tempeh Bolognese

WEEKLY SHOPPING LIST 02

FRUIT & VEGETABLES

Fresh
- ○ 5x onions
- ○ 1x zucchini
- ○ 2x aubergines
- ○ 2x red bell peppers
- ○ 2x bulbs garlic
- ○ spinach
- ○ 1x avocado
- ○ 2x bananas
- ○ 2x lemons
- ○ 2x carrots
- ○ berries
- ○ green beans
- ○ cherry tomatoes
- ○ baby potatoes
- ○ 3x sweet potatoes
- ○ 1x avocado

Herbs
- ○ 2x bunches coriander
- ○ chives
- ○ 1x bunch basil
- ○ 1x bunch parsley
- ○ _____
- ○ _____
- ○ _____
- ○ _____
- ○ _____
- ○ _____

NON-DAIRY & CONDIMENTS

Non-Dairy
- ○ almond milk
- ○ tempeh
- ○ vegan cheese
- ○ coconut yogurt

Cans & Condiments
- ○ 2x cans chickpeas
- ○ peanut butter
- ○ almond butter
- ○ green olives
- ○ sundried tomatoes
- ○ capers
- ○ wholegrain mustard
- ○ apple cider vinegar
- ○ 1x can kidney bens
- ○ 3x cans chickpeas
- ○ tahini
- ○ 2x cans chopped tomatoes
- ○ tomato puree
- ○ 2x cans black beans
- ○ _____
- ○ _____
- ○ _____
- ○ _____
- ○ _____
- ○ _____
- ○ _____

GRAINS, SEEDS & BAKING

Grains
- ○ rolled oats
- ○ oat milk
- ○ quinoa
- ○ pasta

Nuts & Seeds
- ○ sesame seeds

Baking
- ○ oat flour
- ○ coconut flour
- ○ baking powder
- ○ baking soda
- ○ almond meal
- ○ desiccated coconut
- ○ raw cacao
- ○ _____
- ○ _____
- ○ _____
- ○ _____
- ○ _____
- ○ _____
- ○ _____
- ○ _____
- ○ _____

SPICES & MISC.

Spices
- ○ turmeric
- ○ paprika
- ○ cinnamon
- ○ nutmeg
- ○ rosemary
- ○ chili flakes
- ○ mixed herbs
- ○ cumin
- ○ smoked paprika

Oils
- ○ olive oil
- ○ coconut oil

Sweeteners
- ○ maple syrup
- ○ coconut sugar

Other
- ○ vegan vanilla protein powder
- ○ vegan chocolate protein powder
- ○ matcha powder
- ○ _____
- ○ _____
- ○ _____
- ○ _____
- ○ _____
- ○ _____
- ○ _____

GREEK CHICKPEAS ON TOAST

GREEK CHICKPEAS ON TOAST

Serves: 4
Prep: 5 mins
Cook: 20 mins

Nutrition per
serving:
253 kcal
8g Fats
33g Carbs
11g Protein

DF MP
V   Q

Chop it up vegan style

WHAT YOU NEED

- 2 tsp. olive oil
- 2 shallots, diced
- 2 cloves garlic, minced
- ½ tsp. smoked paprika
- ½ tsp. sweet paprika
- ½ tsp. brown sugar
- 1 can (14oz./400g) chopped tomatoes
- 1 can (14oz./400g) chickpeas, drained
- 4 slices bread, toasted
- handful parsley, to garnish
- ⅓ cup (60g) olives, halved, to garnish

WHAT YOU NEED TO DO

Heat the olive oil over medium-high heat on a medium pan. Add shallots and cook for 2-3 minutes, then add garlic and cook for another 1-2 minutes.

Add all the spices to the pan and mix well. Next add in the chopped tomatoes and 2 tbsp. of water. Simmer on low-medium heat until the sauce has reduced, around 10 minutes.

Mix in the drained chickpeas, season with salt, sugar and black pepper and cook for another 5 minutes until warmed through.

Serve on the toasted bread with parsley and black olives.

CHICKPEA SCRAMBLE

CHICKPEA SCRAMBLE

Serves: 2
Prep: 10 mins
Cook: 10 mins

Nutrition per
serving:
417 kcal
15g Fats
56g Carbs
19g Protein

GF DF
V Q

chop it up vegan style

WHAT YOU NEED

- 2 cups (330g) canned chickpeas, drained
- ½ tsp. turmeric
- ½ tsp. paprika
- 2 tsp. olive oil
- 1 small onion, finely diced
- 2 cloves garlic, minced
- ½ tsp. paprika
- 8 oz. (230g) spinach
- ½ avocado

WHAT YOU NEED TO DO

Mash the chickpeas with a fork, leaving some whole. Mix in the turmeric and paprika, and season with salt and pepper.

Heat the oil in a pan over medium-high heat and sauté the onion and garlic for 2-3 minutes, until fragrant.

Next, add in the mashed chickpeas and cook for another 5 minutes, then transfer to a bowl, cover with tin foil and set aside. Using the same pan wilt the spinach, adding a tablespoon of water.

Once ready, divide the spinach between 2 bowls, top with the chickpeas and serve with ¼ avocado.

BANANA
BREAKFAST OATS

BANANA BREAKFAST OATS

Serves: 2
Prep: 5 mins
Cook: 0 mins

Nutrition per
serving:
381 kcal
12g Fats
60g Carbs
10g Protein

DF   MP

V   Q

Chop it up vegan style

WHAT YOU NEED

- 1 cup (90g) oats
- 2 ripe bananas, mashed
- 2 tbsp. peanut butter
- favorite nuts and seeds, to garnish
- seasonal fruit, to garnish

WHAT YOU NEED TO DO

Divide oats between two bowls and add 3 tbsp. of water into each bowl.

Add in one mashed up banana into each bowl and mix well to combine. Set aside for 10 minutes for the oats to soften.

Drizzle the oats with peanut butter and serve with the nuts and seeds and chopped fruit.

NOTE: garnishes (nuts, seeds, fruit) are not included in the nutrition information.

BANANA & STRAWBERRY PANCAKES

BANANA & STRAWBERRY PANCAKES

Serves: 4
Prep: 15 mins
Cook: 15 mins

Nutrition per serving:
282 kcal
53g Fats
7g Carbs
5g Protein

DF LC

MP V

N

Chop it up vegan style

WHAT YOU NEED

- 2 ripe bananas, mashed
- 1 cup (110g) spelt flour
- 1 tsp. baking powder
- ½ tsp. baking soda
- 1 tsp. lemon juice
- ¾ cup (180ml) almond milk
- ¾ cup (150g) strawberries, sliced
- 1 tbsp. coconut oil
- 4 tbsp. coconut yogurt
- 4 tbsp. maple syrup

WHAT YOU NEED TO DO

Mash the banana with a fork and combine them with the flour, baking powder, baking soda, and lemon juice. Next, slowly add in almond milk until you get a thick batter.

Finally, fold in the sliced strawberries, leaving some for garnish.

Heat some of the oil in a non-stick pan over medium heat, not too hot as then the pancakes will burn. Spoon a little less than ¼ cup of the batter per pancake (this will make around 8 pancakes).

Cook the pancakes for about 3 minutes on one side, then when bubbles start to appear flip and cook for another minute.

Serve the pancakes with a tablespoon of coconut yogurt and maple syrup, and garnish with remaining strawberries.

Nutrition information is per 2 pancakes.

CARROT PANCAKES
WITH ALMOND CARAMEL

CARROT PANCAKES WITH ALMOND CARAMEL

Makes: 9
Prep: 20 mins
Cook: 30 mins

Nutrition per 2
pancakes:
363 kcal
12g Fats
57g Carbs
8g Protein

Chop it up vegan style

WHAT YOU NEED

For pancakes:
- 1 rounded cup (140g) oat flour
- 1 tsp. cinnamon
- ¼ tsp. ground ginger
- ¼ tsp. ground nutmeg
- 1¼ tsp. baking powder
- ½ tsp. baking soda
- ¾ cup (180ml) oat milk
- 2 tbsp. almond butter
- 2 tsp. lemon juice
- 2 tbsp. maple syrup
- 1 cup (110g) carrots, grated
- 1 tbsp. coconut oil

For almond caramel:
- ¼ cup (60ml) maple syrup
- 2 tbsp. almond butter
- pinch salt

WHAT YOU NEED TO DO

In a bowl, combine flour, spices, baking powder and baking soda. Whisk in the almond milk, almond butter, lemon juice and maple syrup. Then add in the grated carrots and mix well.

Heat up a non-stick frying pan over medium heat and grease it lightly with some of the coconut oil.

Ladle 2 tablespoons of the pancake mix per pancake. Cook each pancake for about 2 minutes on one side, then flip and another 1-2 minutes on the other side.

Serve with almond caramel sauce.

To make the almond caramel:
Heat up the maple syrup in a small pot over low heat. When it starts to boil gently, take it off the heat and stir in the almond butter with a pinch of salt.

Return the pan on the heat and simmer, stirring the caramel for another minute until thickened. Serves as a pancake topping.

PROTEIN BERRY
SMOOTHIE BOWL

PROTEIN BERRY SMOOTHIE BOWL

Serves: 1
Prep: 5 mins
Cook: 0 mins

Nutrition per
serving:
297 kcal
2g Fats
49g Carbs
23g Protein

GF DF
HP Q

Chop it up vegan style

WHAT YOU NEED

- 1 cup (150g) frozen red berries
- 1 small banana, frozen
- ¼ cup (60ml) coconut milk
- 1 scoop vanilla vegan protein powder

WHAT YOU NEED TO DO

Place frozen berries and banana in a high-speed blender or food processor and blitz on low for about 30 seconds.

Add the milk and protein powder, and blend on low again, scraping down sides as needed, until the mixture reaches a soft-serve consistency. Add more milk if necessary, to reach desired consistency.

Transfer into a serving bowl and top with favorite toppings.

NOTE: toppings are not included in nutrition information.

BREAKFAST
OAT COOKIES

BREAKFAST OAT COOKIES

Makes: 9
Prep: 10 mins
Cook: 20 mins

Nutrition per serving:
137 kcal
6g Fats
17g Carbs
3g Protein

Chop it up vegan style

WHAT YOU NEED

- 1 cup (90g) rolled oats
- ⅓ cup (30g) almond meal
- 3 tbsp. desiccated coconut
- 1 tsp. cinnamon
- ¼ tsp. baking soda
- 3 tbsp. almond butter
- 3 tbsp. maple syrup
- 1 medium ripe banana, mashed
- handful fresh berries

WHAT YOU NEED TO DO

Preheat the oven to 320° F (160°C) and line a baking tray with baking paper.

Place all the ingredients (apart from the berries) in a medium bowl and mix well, then place the mixture in the freezer for 10-15 minutes.

Using slightly wet hands, create 9 balls out of the mixture and place them on the baking tray and push them down to create cookie shapes. Gently press a few berries onto each cookie.

Bake for 20 minutes until golden and allow to cool completely before eating.

GREEN PEA &
MINT DIP

GREEN PEA & MINT DIP

Serves: 4
Prep: 15 mins
Cook: 0 mins

Nutrition per serving:
92 kcal
4g Fats
11g Carbs
4g Protein

GF DF
LC V
Q

Chop it up vegan style

WHAT YOU NEED

- 1 ⅔ cups (250g) green peas, frozen
- 1 clove garlic
- 2 tbsp. lemon juice
- ½ avocado
- 2-3 sprigs fresh mint, leaves only

WHAT YOU NEED TO DO

Place frozen peas in a bowl and cover with boiling water. Let them stand for a few minutes until defrosted, then drain and transfer to a food processor or high speed blender.

Add in the garlic, lemon juice, avocado, mint leaves, and season with salt and pepper. Blend until smooth. Add 1-2 tbsp. of cold water if the dip is too thick. Taste and adjust seasoning to your taste.

Serve as a dip with fresh vegetables, crisps, crackers or pita.

SUNDRIED TOMATO HUMMUS

SUNDRIED TOMATO HUMMUS

Serves: 4
Prep: 5 mins
Cook: 0 mins

Nutrition per
serving:
181 kcal
10g Fats
18g Carbs
6g Protein

Chop it up vegan style

WHAT YOU NEED

- 1½ cups (250g) chickpeas, drained
- ¼ cup (45g) sundried tomatoes in oil
- 1 clove garlic
- ½ lemon, juiced
- 2 tbsp. olive oil
- ½ teaspoon salt
- ¼ cup (60ml) water

WHAT YOU NEED TO DO

Add all the ingredients, except for the water, into a food processor and blend until creamy, stopping once to scrape down the sides.

Check for texture and consistency and add water as necessary. Serve with raw veggies, crackers, or chips.

BABA GHANOUSH

BABA GHANOUSH

Serves: 6
Prep: 20 mins
Cook: 35 mins

Nutrition per
serving:
154 kcal
10g Fats
12g Carbs
5g Protein

WHAT YOU NEED

- 2 medium aubergine
- 2 cloves garlic, crushed
- 1 lemon, juiced
- 4 tbsp. tahini
- 2 tbsp. olive oil
- ½ tsp. ground cumin
- smoked paprika
- 1 tbsp. parsley, chopped

WHAT YOU NEED TO DO

Preheat the oven to 450°F (230°C). Line a large baking tray with baking paper.

Halve the aubergines lengthwise and brush the cut sides lightly with olive oil. Place them in the prepared tray with the halved sides down, roasting them for 35-40 minutes until the flesh is very tender.

Once aubergines are cooked, set them aside to cool, then scoop out the flesh with a spoon, discarding the skin.

Place the flesh on a sieve and leave for a bit (the longer, the better) to allow all the excess liquid to drain away.

Place the flesh in a bowl, add the garlic, lemon juice, tahini, olive oil, and cumin. Mash everything with a fork, and continue stirring and mashing until the mixture is creamy—season to taste with salt.

Transfer to a serving bowl and sprinkle with smoked paprika and chopped parsley to garnish.

Chop it up vegan style

QUINOA TABBOULEH

QUINOA TABBOULEH

Serves: 4
Prep: 10 mins
Cook: 15 mins

Nutrition per serving:
272 kcal
10g Fats
42g Carbs
8g Protein

GF DF
MP V
Q

Chop it up vegan style

WHAT YOU NEED

- 1 cup (170g) quinoa
- 2 medium tomatoes, finely diced
- 1 small cucumber, finely diced
- 1 bell pepper, finely diced
- 1 red onion, finely diced
- ⅔ cup (15g) parsley, chopped
- ⅔ cup (15g) mint, chopped
- juice of 2 limes
- 2 tbsp. olive oil

WHAT YOU NEED TO DO

Cook the quinoa according to instructions on the packaging. Once cooked, place in a large salad bowl.

Finely dice the vegetables and chop the fresh herbs, then add to the salad bowl.

Squeeze in the lime juice, drizzle with olive oil and season to taste with salt and pepper. Mix everything well until combined.

Serves as a salad or side dish. Store covered and refrigerated for up to 3 days.

**GREEN BEANS &
CHERRY TOMATO SALAD**

GREEN BEANS & CHERRY TOMATO SALAD

Serves: 4
Prep: 15 mins
Cook: 5 mins

Nutrition per
serving:
163 kcal
14g Fats
10g Carbs
2g Protein

GF   DF

LC   MP

V   Q

Chop it up vegan style

WHAT YOU NEED

- 1 lb. (450g) green beans
- 1 cup (150g) cherry tomatoes

For the dressing:
- 1 clove garlic, minced
- ⅓ cup (15g) coriander, chopped
- 2 tbsp. lemon juice
- ¼ cup (60ml) olive oil

WHAT YOU NEED TO DO

Trim the stem end of the green beans. Bring water to a boil in a large pot, and cook the beans for 3 minutes. Then drain and rinse with cold water, allowing them to cool completely.

Half the cherry tomatoes and place in a salad bowl. Once beans are cool cut them in 1-2 inch pieces and add to the salad bowl.

Make the dressing by placing the dressing ingredients in a food processor. Pulse until a smooth sauce has formed. Season to taste with salt and pepper.

Add the sauce to the green beans and tomatoes and mix well until coated. Serve immediately as a salad or side dish. Store covered in the fridge for 2-3 days.

VEGAN 'TUNA' SALAD

VEGAN 'TUNA' SALAD

Serves: 1
Prep: 10 mins
Cook: 0 mins

Nutrition per
serving:
255 kcal
9g Fats
35g Carbs
10g Protein

GF DF
MP V
Q

Chop it up vegan style

WHAT YOU NEED

- 2 ½ cups (400g) chickpeas, drained
- 2 nori sheets
- 2 tbsp. vegan mayo (or tahini)
- 2 tbsp. lemon juice
- 1 cup (175g) sweetcorn, drained
- 1 small onion, finely diced

WHAT YOU NEED TO DO

Place chickpeas in a bowl and mash them with a fork, leaving some bigger parts for more texture.

Blend the nori sheet in a high-speed blender until you get nori flakes. And add it to the chickpeas. Add the rest of the ingredients and stir until well combined.

Serve on its own, or a filling for sandwiches and jacket potatoes. Store in the fridge for up to 4-5 days.

POTATO & SUNDRIED TOMATO SALAD

POTATO & SUNDRIED TOMATO SALAD

Serves: 4
Prep: 10 mins
Cook: 20 mins

Nutrition per serving:
161 kcal
9g Fats
17g Carbs
4g Protein

GF DF
LC MP
V

Chop it up vegan style

WHAT YOU NEED

- 1 lb. (450g) baby potatoes
- ½ cup (90g) green olives, halved
- ½ cup (70g) sundried tomatoes, drained, roughly chopped
- 2 tbsp. capers, drained
- handful chives, chopped
- 1 tbsp. oil from sundried tomatoes
- 1 tbsp. wholegrain mustard
- 1 tbsp. apple cider vinegar

WHAT YOU NEED TO DO

Place the potatoes in a pot of salted water and bring to a boil, lower the heat and simmer for about 20 minutes. Once cooked, drain and rinse in cold water. Once slightly cooled, peel, halve and place them in a bowl.

Add in the olives, sundried tomatoes, capers, and chives. Next, mix the oil for the tomatoes, mustard, and apple cider vinegar and drizzle over the salad. Season to taste with salt and pepper, mix well and serve.

WILD RICE, TOMATO &
ROCKET BALSAMIC SALAD

WILD RICE, TOMATO & ROCKET BALSAMIC SALAD

Serves: 4
Prep: 10 mins
Cook: 20 mins

Nutrition per serving:
288 kcal
9g Fats
44g Carbs
7g Protein

Chop it up vegan style

WHAT YOU NEED

- 1 cup (185g) rice
- 160g roasted peppers, drained, chopped
- ¼ cup (30g) roasted almonds, chopped
- 1 cup (150g) cherry tomatoes, halved
- 2 oz. (60g) rocket
- 1 tbsp. balsamic vinegar
- 1 tbsp. olive oil
- ½ tsp. chili flakes

WHAT YOU NEED TO DO

Cook the rice according to instructions on the packaging. Once cooked, place in a large bowl.

Add in the peppers, almonds, tomatoes, and rocket. Drizzle with vinegar and oil, add chili flakes—season to taste with salt and pepper and mix until well combined, before serving.

SWEET POTATO, QUINOA & BEAN BURGER

SWEET POTATO, QUINOA & BEAN BURGER

Makes: 4
Prep: 10 mins
Cook: 55 mins

Nutrition per serving:
171 kcal
6g Fats
22g Carbs
5g Protein

GF DF
MP V

Chop it up vegan style

WHAT YOU NEED

- 1 sweet potato
- ⅓ cup (60g) quinoa, raw
- 14 oz. (400g) can kidney beans, drained
- 1 tsp. rosemary
- ½ tsp. chili flakes
- 1 ½ tbsp. olive oil

WHAT YOU NEED TO DO

Preheat oven to 410°F (210°C) and cut the sweet potato into ¾ inch (2cm) pieces. Place it in an ovenproof dish, drizzle with ½ tbsp. olive oil and season with salt & pepper, rosemary, and chili flakes. Bake for 25-30 minutes.

Once potatoes are cooked, allow them to cool slightly. Then peel off the skin, place in a bowl, and mash the flesh with a fork. Add in the drained beans and also mash with a fork.

Cook quinoa according to instructions on the packaging. Once cooked, transfer to the mashed beans and potato, season with salt & pepper, and mix well.

Using slightly wet hands, form 4 burgers and grease each one with the remaining olive oil. Place on a baking tray lined with tin foil and bake for 20-25 minutes in 410°F (210°C).

CURRIED TOFU SALAD

CURRIED TOFU SALAD

Serves: 4
Prep: 15 mins
Cook: 0 mins

Nutrition per serving:
178 kcal
13g Fats
11g Carbs
6g Protein

Chop it up vegan style

WHAT YOU NEED

- 7 oz. (200g) tofu, drained, crumbled
- 2 celery sticks, chopped
- 1 small onion, diced
- ¼ cup (30g) almonds, chopped
- ¼ cup (30g) raisins
- 3 tbsp. vegan mayonnaise
- 1 tsp. curry powder
- 1 tbsp. dill, chopped

WHAT YOU NEED TO DO

Crumble the tofu into a bowl. Add in the rest of the ingredients, season with salt & pepper, and stir well to combine.

Store in the fridge for up to 4-5 days.

ROASTED MISO
POTATOES

ROASTED MISO POTATOES

Serves: 4
Prep: 10 mins
Cook: 30 mins

Nutrition per
serving:
220 kcal
6g Fats
38g Carbs
4g Protein

GF DF
MP V
N

Chop it up vegan style

WHAT YOU NEED

- 21 oz. (600g) sweet potato
- 1 tbsp. olive oil
- handful coriander, chopped
- 2 tbsp. almonds, chopped

For the sauce:
- 2 tbsp. white miso paste
- 1 tbsp. rice vinegar
- 1 tbsp. maple syrup
- 2 tsp. sriracha
- 1 tbsp. soy yogurt

WHAT YOU NEED TO DO

Preheat oven to 425°F (220°C).

Wash the potatoes and cut them into wedges. Place them on a baking tray and drizzle with olive oil. Season with salt & pepper. Cook for 30 minutes or until soft and charred.

In the meantime, combine all the sauce ingredients in a small bowl.

Once potatoes are cooked, arrange them on a serving dish, drizzle with the sauce and top with chopped almonds and coriander.

ROASTED SWEET POTATO,
KALE & QUINOA SALAD

ROASTED SWEET POTATO, KALE & QUINOA SALAD

Serves: 4
Prep: 20 mins
Cook: 40 mins

Nutrition per
serving:
224 kcal
8g Fats
33g Carbs
6g Protein

GF DF
MP V

Chop it up vegan style

WHAT YOU NEED

- 2 medium sweet potatoes, chopped into cubes
- 2 tbsp. olive oil
- ½ cup (85g) quinoa, uncooked
- 1 red onion, cut into wedges
- 2 cloves garlic, minced
- 1 bunch curly kale, de-stemmed and torn into pieces
- 2 tbsp. balsamic vinegar
- 1 tsp. thyme

WHAT YOU NEED TO DO

Preheat oven to 400°F (200°C).

Place sweet potatoes in baking dish and drizzle with 1 tbsp. oil. Season to taste with salt and pepper. Bake in the oven for 25-30 minutes until tender. Then set aside to cool.

In the meantime, cook quinoa according to instructions on the packaging. Once cooked, set aside to cool.

Meanwhile, heat the remaining 1 tbsp. of oil in a large skillet over medium heat. Cook the onion and garlic, for about 10 minutes, until golden brown.

Stir in the kale and continue cooking until wilted. Transfer the kale mixture to a large bowl and set aside to cool.

Once all the ingredients have cooled, add in the sweet potatoes and quinoa to the large bowl. Drizzle with balsamic vinegar and season to taste with salt and ground pepper. Stir to combine and serve.

**RED SWEET
POTATO CURRY**

RED SWEET POTATO CURRY

Serves: 4
Prep: 10 mins
Cook: 35 mins

Nutrition per
serving:
459 kcal
18g Fats
62g Carbs
13g Protein

WHAT YOU NEED

- 2 tsp. coconut oil
- 1 white onion, diced
- 2 cloves garlic, minced
- 4 tbsp. Thai red curry paste
- 2 sweet potatoes, peeled and diced
- 14oz. (400g) can chopped tomatoes
- 1 cup (240ml) vegetable stock
- ¼ cup (65g) smooth natural peanut butter
- ½ cup (120ml) canned coconut milk, light
- juice of 1 lime
- 3 cups (480g) cooked white rice
- ¼ cup (30g) peanuts, chopped
- handful coriander, chopped

WHAT YOU NEED TO DO

Heat the coconut oil over medium heat in large pan. Add the onion and cook for around 5 minutes until soft.

Next add the garlic and red curry paste and stir well. Add the sweet potatoes, chopped tomatoes, vegetable broth, and season with salt and pepper. Bring to a boil, then reduce the heat to medium-low and simmer for 30 to 35 minutes until the sweet potatoes are tender.

In a small bowl, whisk together the peanut butter and coconut milk. Pour into the pan and stir well to combine.

Remove from the heat, squeeze in lime juice, mix well and serve with the cooked rice. Garnish with the chopped peanuts and coriander.

Chop it up vegan style

GARLIC ZUCCHINI & TOMATO PASTA

GARLIC ZUCCHINI & TOMATO PASTA

Serves: 4
Prep: 5 mins
Cook: 10 mins

Nutrition per serving:
276 kcal
7g Fats
48g Carbs
8g Protein

Chop it up vegan style

WHAT YOU NEED

- 4 cups (220g) brown rice pasta, cooked
- 2 medium zucchini, spiralized
- 1 tbsp. olive oil
- 1 cup (150g) cherry tomatoes, halved
- 2 cloves garlic, crushed
- 1 tsp. smoked paprika
- chili flakes, to taste
- 2 tsp. parsley dried
- 4 tbsp. vegan parmesan, grated (optional)

WHAT YOU NEED TO DO

Cook the pasta according to instructions on the packaging.

Heat olive oil over medium heat in a pan and sauté the zucchini and cherry tomatoes for 2-3 minutes. Season with salt and pepper, add in the crushed garlic and cook for another 2 minutes.

Add in the cooked pasta and mix well—season with smoked paprika and chili flakes.

Divide between bowls and top with vegan parmesan cheese and dried parsley.

SESAME TEMPEH STIR-FRY

SESAME TEMPEH STIR-FRY

Serves: 4
Prep: 10 mins
Cook: 20 mins

Nutrition per
serving:
507 kcal
13g Fats
54g Carbs
17g Protein

DF   MP

V

Chop it up vegan style

WHAT YOU NEED

- 7 oz. (200g) tempeh, cut into cubes
- 1 tbsp. olive oil
- 1 tbsp. ginger, grated
- 2 cloves garlic, crushed
- 1 tbsp. sesame oil
- 1 tbsp. rice wine vinegar
- 3 tbsp. tamari (or soy sauce)
- 2 tbsp. maple syrup
- 2 carrots, chopped or cut into thin strips
- ½ broccoli head, florets
- 1 bell pepper, sliced
- 1 tbsp. sesame seeds, to garnish
- spring onion or chives, to garnish
- 3 cups (585g), brown rice, cooked

WHAT YOU NEED TO DO

Heat the olive oil in a pan over medium-high heat and cook the tempeh for about 6 minutes, occasionally stirring until browned on each side.

In the meantime, prepare the sauce by mixing ginger, garlic, sesame oil, rice wine vinegar, soy sauce, and maple syrup in a bowl.

Add half the sauce to the pan with the tempeh, mix until coated, then remove it from the pan and set it aside.

Add the carrots, broccoli and pepper, and remaining sauce to the pan and cook for about 5 minutes, or until veggies are tender.

Next, add in the tempeh and cook for another 3-5 minutes or until the vegetables are cooked through.

Once ready, serve with ¾ cup cooked brown rice, sesame seeds, and sliced spring onion or chives.

AUBERGINE & TOMATO PASTA

AUBERGINE & TOMATO PASTA

Serves: 4
Prep: 10 mins
Cook: 30 mins

Nutrition per
serving:
459 kcal
11g Fats
76g Carbs
14g Protein

DF MP

V

Chop it up vegan style

WHAT YOU NEED

- 3 cups (300g) pasta, uncooked
- 2 aubergines, cut into bite-size pieces
- 1 tbsp. olive oil
- 1 tbsp. oil from sundried tomatoes
- 14 oz. (400g) can chopped tomatoes
- 10 sundried tomatoes, drained
- 3 cloves garlic, minced
- 1 onion, diced
- 2 tbsp. tomato puree
- 1 tsp. coconut sugar
- 2 tsp. mixed herbs

WHAT YOU NEED TO DO

Preheat the oven to 375°F (190°C). Cook pasta according to instructions on the packaging.

Place the cut aubergine on a baking tray lined with baking paper and drizzle with 1 tbsp. of oil. Season with salt and cook in the oven for 35 minutes, until soft.

While the aubergine is cooking, heat 1 tbsp. of the sundried tomato oil in a pan over medium heat. Sauté the onion and garlic for around 5 minutes.

Next, add in the tomato puree, mixed herbs, and sundried tomatoes. Mix well and continue cooking for 2 minutes. Then add the chopped tomatoes and sugar. Reduce the heat and simmer until the aubergine is ready.

Once pasta and aubergine are ready, mix everything, and serve.

VEG & TAHINI TRAY BAKE

VEG & TAHINI TRAY BAKE

Serves: 4
Prep: 10 mins
Cook: 35 mins

Nutrition per
serving:
260 kcal
13g Fats
26g Carbs
11g Protein

GF DF
MP N

Chop it up vegan style

WHAT YOU NEED

- 1 onion, sliced
- 1 zucchini, sliced
- 1 red bell pepper, sliced
- 1 cup (265g) chickpeas, drained
- 1 tbsp. olive oil
- 3 tbsp. tahini
- 1 lemon, juice only
- 3 tbsp. almond milk
- 1 tbsp. sesame seeds
- handful coriander, chopped

WHAT YOU NEED TO DO

Preheat oven to 190°C (375°F).

Place the chopped vegetables in a baking tray, drizzle with olive oil and season with salt and pepper. Mix well and cook in the oven for 35 minutes or until vegetables are cooked.

In a small bowl, mix the tahini, lemon juice, milk, and sesame seeds, then set aside.

Once vegetables are cooked, mix them with the tahini sauce and serve with fresh coriander.

TEMPEH BOLOGNESE

TEMPEH BOLOGNESE

Serves: 4
Prep: 10 mins
Cook: 45 mins

Nutrition per
serving:
413 kcal
10g Fats
62g Carbs
19g Protein

Chop it up vegan style

WHAT YOU NEED

- 8 oz. (225g) penne, uncooked
- 1 tbsp. olive oil
- 3 cloves garlic, minced
- 1 medium onion, chopped
- 1 red bell pepper, chopped
- 7 oz. (200g) tempeh, crumbled
- 14 oz. (400g) can chopped tomatoes
- 2 tbsp. tomato puree
- 1 tbsp. apple vinegar
- 1 tsp. mixed herbs
- fresh basil, for serving

WHAT YOU NEED TO DO

Cook pasta according to instructions on the packaging.

Heat olive oil over medium-high heat in a large pan. Add garlic and onion and sauté until fragrant, for about 3-4 minutes. Add in bell pepper and crumbled tempeh and sauté for another 5 minutes.

Reduce heat to medium-low and add chopped tomatoes, tomato puree, vinegar and mixed herbs – season with salt and pepper. Bring to boil and let it simmer for 5-6 minutes or until heated through.

To serve, divide pasta and Bolognese between plates and garnish with basil.

TOFU PAD THAI

TOFU PAD THAI

Serves: 4
Prep: 15 mins
Cook: 15 mins

Nutrition per
serving:
469 kcal
18g Fats
68g Carbs
15g Protein

GF MP
V   N

Chop it up vegan style

WHAT YOU NEED

For the sauce:
- ¼ cup (60ml) tamari
- ¼ cup (60ml) maple syrup
- 3 tbsp. water
- 2 tbsp. rice vinegar
- 2 tbsp. peanut butter
- 1 tbsp. sriracha

For the tofu:
- 7 oz. (200g) firm tofu, cubed
- 1 tbsp. flour
- 1 tbsp. coconut oil

For the Pad Thai:
- 8 oz. (225g) thick rice noodles
- 1 tbsp. coconut oil
- 2 shallots, chopped
- 2 large carrots, sliced into ribbons or matchsticks
- 3 cloves garlic, minced
- 2 handfuls bean sprouts
- 3 spring onions, sliced (green part)
- ¼ cup (30g) peanuts, chopped, to serve
- 1 lime, cut into wedges

WHAT YOU NEED TO DO

Mix all the sauce ingredients in a bowl and set aside.

In a large bowl, toss the tofu with flour and season with salt making sure all sides are coated and set aside.

Cook the noodles according to instructions on the packaging.

Heat the coconut oil in a wok or large skillet over medium-high heat. Add the prepared tofu cubes and cook for 1-2 minutes until brown. Remove from heat and set aside.

Now add the shallots, carrots, and garlic to the wok. Stir fry for 1-2 minutes until softened, add in the earlier prepared sauce and noodles, and cook for 1 minute.

Next, add in the tofu and bean sprouts, and gently mix until well combined. Remove from heat and top with the green part of the spring onions. Serve with peanuts and lime wedges.

PRESSING TOFU:
Wrap a block of tofu in a few paper towels and place it on a plate. Place a cast-iron skillet on top (or something heavy) and let it drain for about 15 minutes or more. Pat dry to remove excess moisture on the surface.

QUICK VEGETABLE
STIR FRY

QUICK VEGETABLE STIR FRY

Serves: 4
Prep: 10 mins
Cook: 15 mins

Nutrition per
serving:
273 kcal
8g Fats
45g Carbs
6g Protein

GF DF
MP V
Q

Chop it up vegan style

WHAT YOU NEED

For the sauce:
- 1 tbsp. tahini
- 1 tbsp. toasted sesame oil
- 1 tsp. white miso paste
- 1 lime, juiced

For the stir-fry:
- 6 ⅓ oz. (180g) rice noodles
- 1 tsp. toasted sesame oil
- 1 large carrot, spiralized
- 1 zucchini, spiralized
- ½ cup green peas, frozen
- 1 tbsp. sesame seeds
- coriander, to serve

WHAT YOU NEED TO DO

Mix all the sauce ingredients.

Cook noodles according to instructions on the packaging, then set aside.

Spiralized the carrot and zucchini. However, if you don't have a spiraliser, then just grate them using the large holes.

Heat 1 tsp. of sesame oil in a large skillet over medium heat. Add in the carrot and zucchini noodles and cook for 3-4 minutes. Next, add in the green peas, sesame seeds, and cooked noodles. Mix well and cook for another 3-4 minutes.

Finally, add in the sauce and cook for a final 2-3 minutes until warmed through. Serve with fresh coriander.

ROASTED AUBERGINE
AND TOMATO STEW

ROASTED AUBERGINE AND TOMATO STEW

Serves: 4
Prep: 5 mins
Cook: 50 mins

Nutrition per
serving:
260 kcal
9g Fats
34g Carbs
10g Protein

GF DF
MP V

Chop it up vegan style

WHAT YOU NEED

- 2 tbsp. olive oil
- 2 medium aubergines, cut into bite-size pieces
- 2 cups (330g) cherry tomatoes
- 14oz. (400g) can chopped tomatoes
- 14oz. (400g) can chickpeas, drained
- 1 medium onion, chopped
- 2 cloves garlic, chopped
- 4 tbsp. tomato puree
- 1 tbsp. apple cider vinegar
- 2 tsp. mixed herbs
- handful parsley, chopped

WHAT YOU NEED TO DO

Pre-heat the oven to 400°F (200°C). Place the cut aubergine into a baking dish and drizzle with 1 tbsp. olive oil and season with salt. Cook in the oven for 40 minutes until soft.

In the meantime, heat the remaining 1 tbsp. oil in a large skillet over medium heat.

Add the onion and garlic, season with salt and pepper, and cook for 5-6 minutes until soft—then add in the mixed herbs, tomato puree, and cook for another 2 minutes.

Next, add in the chopped tomatoes, vinegar, chickpeas, and cherry tomatoes. Bring to boil, then reduce heat and continue simmering until the aubergine is ready.

Once the aubergine is soft, add into the tomato sauce and mix well. Serve with rice and chopped parsley.

SPICY CAULIFLOWER & CHICKPEA RICE BOWL

SPICY CAULIFLOWER & CHICKPEA RICE BOWL

Serves: 4
Prep: 10 mins
Cook: 25 mins

Nutrition per
serving:
380 kcal
11g Fats
57g Carbs
13g Protein

GF   DF

MP   V

N

Chop it up vegan style

WHAT YOU NEED

- 1 medium cauliflower, broken into florets
- 14 oz. (400g) can chickpeas, drained
- 1 tbsp. olive oil
- 3 cups cooked rice

For the sauce:
- 2 tbsp. sriracha
- 2 tbsp. tamari
- 1 tbsp. maple syrup
- 2 tsp. apple cider vinegar
- 2 tsp. fresh ginger, minced
- 2 cloves garlic, minced
- 1 tsp. sesame oil
- 2 green onions, chopped
- ¼ cup (30g) peanuts, chopped

WHAT YOU NEED TO DO

Preheat oven to 230°C (450°F) and prepare a baking dish or tray.

Break the cauliflower into bite-size florets and place them on the tray along with drained chickpeas. Drizzle with olive oil and season to taste with sea salt and pepper—bake in the oven for 20 minutes.

In the meantime, prepare the sauce by mixing all the sauce ingredients in a small bowl.

Once cauliflower and chickpeas are roasted, remove from oven and mix with the earlier prepared sauce.

Increase the oven temperature to broil, return the tray into the oven and cook for about another 5 minutes.

Remove from the oven divide between bowls and serve with a portion of rice.

SWEET POTATO & BEAN BAKE

SWEET POTATO & BEAN BAKE

Serves: 4
Prep: 30 mins
Cook: 75 mins

Nutrition per
serving:
361 kcal
17g Fats
44g Carbs
9g Protein

GF   DF
MP   V

Chop it up vegan style

WHAT YOU NEED

- 2 large sweet potatoes, peeled
- 2x 14 oz. (400g) cans black beans, drained
- 7 oz. (200g) vegan cheese, grated
- handful parsley, chopped

For the sauce:
- 1 tbsp. olive oil,
- 1 onion, diced
- 3 cloves garlic, minced
- 1 tsp. ground cumin, more to season layers
- 2 tsp. smoked paprika, more to season layers
- 1 tsp. mixed herbs, more to season layers
- 14 oz. (400g) can chopped tomatoes
- ¼ cup (60ml) tomato puree

WHAT YOU NEED TO DO

Firstly, prepare the tomato sauce. Heat the olive oil in a large pan over medium-high heat.

Add the diced onion and garlic and fry until fragrant, 3-4 minutes. Next, add in the spices and herbs and cook for another minute, stirring.

Add in the chopped tomatoes and tomato puree, and season with salt and pepper to taste. Bring to boil and then reduce heat to low and simmer for 15-20 minutes until the sauce is reduced and thickens.

Preheat the oven to 355°F (180°C). Spread half of the tomato at the bottom of a baking dish.

Slice the sweet potatoes into 0.1" (3mm) thin slices and try to make each slice the same thickness.

Place a layer of sweet potato on the tomato sauce overlapping slightly—season with salt, herbs, and smoked paprika.

Next, spread 1 can of black beans on top of the potato. Follow with another layer of sweet potato, and season with salt, herbs, and smoked paprika. Spread the second can of black beans followed with a third layer of sweet potato. Again season with salt, herbs, and smoked paprika.

Finally, top with the remaining tomato sauce. Cover with a piece of tin foil and bake for about 40-50 minutes, until the sweet potato is cooked through.

Sprinkle with grated vegan cheese and bake without cover for another 10-15 minutes, until the cheese has melted.

PRE-WORKOUT OAT & BANANA SMOOTHIE

PRE-WORKOUT OAT & BANANA SMOOTHIE

Serves: 1
Prep: 5 mins
Cook: 0 mins

Nutrition per
serving:
291 kcal
7g Fats
54g Carbs
6g Protein

Chop it up vegan style

WHAT YOU NEED

- 2 tbsp. rolled oats
- 3 tbsp. hot water
- 1 banana, sliced & frozen
- 1 tbsp. flaxseed meal
- 1 tbsp. maple syrup
- 1 cup (240ml) almond milk, unsweetened

WHAT YOU NEED TO DO

Soak the oats in the water for a few minutes until softened.

Then place all the ingredients in a blender and blitz until smooth. Serve immediately.

POST-WORKOUT CHOCOLATE PROTEIN SMOOTHIE

POST-WORKOUT CHOCOLATE PROTEIN SMOOTHIE

Serves: 1
Prep: 5 mins
Cook: 0 mins

Nutrition per
serving:
401 kcal
20g Fats
38g Carbs
24g Protein

 GF DF
 HP V
 Q N

Chop it up vegan style

WHAT YOU NEED

- 1 banana
- ¼ avocado
- 1 tbsp. almond butter
- 1 tbsp. raw cacao powder
- 2 tbsp. vegan chocolate protein powder
- 1 cup (240ml) almond milk, unsweetened

WHAT YOU NEED TO DO

Place all the ingredients in a blender and blitz until smooth. Serve immediately.

VEGAN NUTELLA

VEGAN NUTELLA

Serves: 16
Prep: 10 mins
Cook: 0 mins

Nutrition per serving:
119 kcal
10g Fats
7g Carbs
3g Protein

Chop it up vegan style

WHAT YOU NEED

- 2 cups (240g) roasted hazelnuts
- 1 tbsp. vanilla extract
- 4 tbsp. cocoa powder
- 4 tbsp. maple syrup
- ¼ tsp. salt
- 2 tsp. coconut oil
- ½ cup (120ml) hazelnut milk (or almond)

WHAT YOU NEED TO DO

Place the roasted hazelnuts in a high-speed blender and blend until ground to tiny pieces.

Add in the rest of the ingredients and blitz again until smooth. You will need to scrape down the edges a few times during this process. Add in additional milk if required to reach a butter-like texture.

ENERGY BALLS

ENERGY BALLS

Makes: 10
Prep: 15 mins
Cook: 0 mins

Nutrition per
serving:
137 kcal
9g Fats
11g Carbs
2g Protein

GF   DF

LC   MP

V   Q

N

Chop it up vegan style

WHAT YOU NEED

- 1 cup (120g) dates, without stone
- ¾ cup (60g) almond meal
- ½ cup (30g) desiccated coconut
- 2 tbsp. chia seeds
- 2 tbsp. coconut oil, melted
- 1 tbsp. natural peanut butter

WHAT YOU NEED TO DO

Place all ingredients in a high-speed blender or food processor and blitz until everything is well combined and chopped to small pieces.

Using your hands, form 10 balls about the size of a walnut. Place them in the fridge to chill for at least 1 hour so that they become more solid.

Store in the fridge in an airtight container for up to 2 weeks.

MATCHA
ENERGY BALLS

MATCHA ENERGY BALLS

Makes: 12
Prep: 10 mins
Cook: 0 mins

Nutrition per
serving:
94 kcal
6g Fats
7g Carbs
2g Protein

Chop it up vegan style

WHAT YOU NEED

- 1 tbsp. matcha powder
- 1 cup (80g) desiccated coconut
- ¼ cup (50g) coconut flour
- 1 scoop (25g) vanilla protein powder (vegan mix)
- 2 tbsp. coconut oil
- 3 tbsp. maple syrup

WHAT YOU NEED TO DO

Add all ingredients into a food processor and pulse until well combined.

Form into 12 balls with your hands and store in the fridge for up to 7 days.

SIMPLE VEGAN
OAT COOKIES

SIMPLE VEGAN OAT COOKIES

Makes: 12
Prep: 15 mins
Cook: 20 mins

Nutrition per
serving:
166 kcal
9g Fats
18g Carbs
4g Protein

Chop it up vegan style

WHAT YOU NEED

- 2 cups (180g) oats
- 1 cup (100g) oat flour
- 5/8 cup (70g) almond meal
- 6 tbsp. maple syrup
- 4 tbsp. coconut oil, melted
- 1 tsp. baking powder

WHAT YOU NEED TO DO

Preheat oven to 360°F (180°C) and line a baking tray with baking paper.

In a bowl, mix the oats, flour, almond meal, baking powder, and a pinch of salt. Add in maple syrup and coconut oil, mix well until combined.

Using slightly wet hands, create 12 balls out of the mixture and place them on the baking tray and push them down to create cookies shapes.

Bake for 20 minutes until golden and allow to cool before eating.

BANANA &
ALMOND MUFFINS

BANANA & ALMOND MUFFINS

Makes: 6
Prep: 10 mins
Cook: 20 mins

Nutrition per
serving:
210 kcal
10g Fats
28g Carbs
5g Protein

Chop it up vegan style

WHAT YOU NEED

- 2 ripe bananas, mashed
- ¼ cup (60ml) maple syrup
- ¼ cup (60ml) almond butter
- ½ cup (55g) spelt flour
- 1 tsp. baking powder
- ¼ tsp. baking soda
- ¼ cup (30g) walnuts

WHAT YOU NEED TO DO

Heat the oven to 355°F (180°C) and line a muffin tray with paper muffin cups.

Mash the bananas with a fork and combine with the maple syrup and almond butter. Fold in the flour, baking powder, and baking soda and mix well.

Divide the batter between the 6 muffin cups. Top each one with the walnuts.

Bake for about 18-20 minutes in the middle of the oven, or until a toothpick comes out clean.

Remove the muffins from the oven and cool completely before serving.

LEMON & BERRY
CHEESECAKE

LEMON & BERRY CHEESECAKE

Serves: 16
Prep: 30 mins
Chill: 2 hrs

Nutrition per
serving:
297 kcal
19g Fats
30g Carbs
5g Protein

GF DF
MP V

N

Chop it up vegan style

WHAT YOU NEED

For the crust:
- ½ cup (40g) desiccated coconut
- 1 cup (100g) walnuts, chopped
- 12 medjool dates
- pinch of salt

For the lemon layer:
- 2 cups (230g) cashews, soaked for 4 hours or overnight
- 1 cup (240ml) coconut cream
- 4 tbsp. coconut oil, soft
- ½ cup (120ml) maple syrup
- zest of 1 lemon
- juice of 1 lemon juice
- pinch of salt

For the berry layer:
- 1 cup (150g) frozen red berries
- 2 tbsp. chia seeds
- 2 tbsp. lemon juice
- 2 tbsp. maple syrup

WHAT YOU NEED TO DO

Place all the crust ingredients into a food processor and blitz until sticky paste forms. Transfer the crust into a cake tin or springform pan and press evenly to form the bottom layer. Place the tin in the freezer while you make the other layers.

Drain the cashews and pat dry with a kitchen towel. Place all the lemon layer ingredients in a food processor and puree until smooth. Spread over the crust and return into the freezer.

Prepare the last berry layer. Place all ingredients in the food processor and puree until smooth. Spread over the top of the cheesecake only when the lemon layer has set completely. Garnish with additional berries (optional). Return to the freezer and freeze until set.

Remove the cheesecake from the freezer for about 20 minutes before serving.

ALMOND &
PEACH CAKE

ALMOND & PEACH CAKE

Serves: 12
Prep: 10 mins
Cook: 50 mins

Nutrition per
serving:
199 kcal
6g Fats
30g Carbs
5g Protein

Chop it up vegan style

WHAT YOU NEED

- 4 tbsp. almond butter
- ½ cup (125g) peach vegan yogurt (like Alpro)
- ½ cup (120ml) almond milk
- ½ cup (120ml) + 2 tbsp. maple syrup
- 1 tbsp. lemon juice
- 2 tsp. vanilla extract
- 2 peaches, cut into 8 segments each
- scant 2 cups (240g) all-purpose flour
- ¾ cup (80g) almond meal
- 1 tsp. baking powder
- ½ tsp. baking soda
- 2 tsp. cinnamon
- 3 tsp. ground ginger

WHAT YOU NEED TO DO

Preheat the oven to 355°F (180°C) and grease (length) round cake tin or line it with baking paper.

In a large bowl, whisk together the almond butter and yogurt until smooth, then gradually add in the almond milk and maple syrup. Finally, mix in the lemon juice and vanilla.

In another bowl, sift flour and add ground almonds, baking powder, baking soda, and spices. Mix well. Fold the dry ingredients into the wet ones, mixing it well with a spatula.

Transfer the batter into the cake tin, and place the peach segments on top. Bake for about 50 minutes or until a toothpick comes out clean.

Glaze the top with the remaining 2 tbsp. of maple syrup and let it cool down completely before serving.

VEGAN CHOCOLATE BROWNIES

VEGAN CHOCOLATE BROWNIES

Makes: 16
Prep: 20 mins
Cook: 35 mins

Nutrition per
serving:
223 kcal
15g Fats
21g Carbs
3g Protein

Chop it up vegan style

WHAT YOU NEED

- 8 oz. (220g) +70% dark chocolate, chopped
- 3 tbsp. coconut oil
- 2 ripe avocados
- 1 cup (200g) coconut palm sugar
- 2 flax eggs
- 1 tsp. vanilla extract
- ¾ cup (75g) almond meal
- ¼ cup (30g) unsweetened cocoa powder
- ½ tsp. baking powder
- ½ teaspoon sea salt
- ½ cup (50g) walnuts, chopped

HOW TO MAKE A FLAX EGG:
To make one flax egg mix 1 tbsp. flaxseed meal and 2 ½ tbsp. water. Let it rest for 5 mins to thicken.

WHAT YOU NEED TO DO

Preheat oven to 350˚F (175˚C).

Line a 8x8-inch baking pan with baking paper.

Place the coconut oil and chopped chocolate in a medium size heatproof bowl. Place the bowl over a pot of lightly simmering water. Stir the chocolate and coconut oil until they are completely melted.

In a large bowl, mash avocado and then stir in the chocolate mixture. Whisk in the sugar, then add in the flax eggs and vanilla extract, mix well.

Next add in the cocoa powder, almond meal, baking powder and salt, mixing until just combined (do not overmix). Finally, stir in chopped walnuts.

Spread the batter into the prepared baking tin and place it in the middle of the oven. Bake for about 25 to 30 minutes until the middle is set.

Let completely cool on a rack and cut into 12 squares.

Printed in the United States
by Baker & Taylor Publisher Services